OCCULT READING AND OCCULT HEARING

RUDOLF STEINER

OCCULT READING
AND
OCCULT HEARING

Four lectures given in Dornach,
3rd to 6th October, 1914

Translated by D. S. Osmond

RUDOLF STEINER PRESS
LONDON

First edition in English 1975

Translated from shorthand reports unrevised by the lecturer. In the complete edition in German of the works of Rudolf Steiner the volume in which the original German texts are included is entitled: *Okkultes Lesen und okkultes Hören* (Bibl. Nr. 156).

This English edition is published by permission of the *Rudolf Steiner-Nachlassverwaltung*, Dornach, Switzerland.

© Rudolf Steiner Press, London, 1975

ISBN 0 85440 286 1

MADE AND PRINTED IN GREAT BRITAIN BY
THE GARDEN CITY PRESS LIMITED
LETCHWORTH, HERTFORDSHIRE
SG6 1JS

The following lectures were given by Rudolf Steiner to audiences familiar with the general background of his anthroposophical teachings. He constantly emphasised the distinction between his written works and reports of lectures which were given as oral communications and were not originally intended for print. It should also be remembered that certain premises were taken for granted when the words were spoken. 'These premises,' Rudolf Steiner writes in his autobiography, 'include at the very least the anthroposophical knowledge of Man and of the Cosmos in its spiritual essence; also of what may be called "anthroposophical history", told as an outcome of research into the spiritual world.'

*   *   *

A brief list of relevant literature in English translation and a summarised plan of the Complete Edition of Rudolf Steiner's works in the original German will be found at the end of the present volume.

CONTENTS

Page

Lecture I
The Human Being and his Relationship to the World   9
3rd October, 1914

Lecture II
Identification with the Signs and Spiritual Realities of the Imaginative World   26
4th October, 1914

Lecture III
Inner Experiences and 'Moods' of Soul as the Vowels and Consonants of the Spiritual World   43
5th October, 1914

Lecture IV
Inner Mobility of Thought   60
6th October, 1914

LECTURE I

The Human Being and his Relationship to the World

You must not expect that these four lectures can be a substitute for those which were planned for Munich.* I will try to give a brief outline of what was to have been the content of the Munich lectures but the most important and essential information that was to have been given there must be reserved for less turbulent times. I am astonished to find certain people thinking that the strenuous efforts required for giving very important teachings of Spiritual Science—as was intended in Munich—can be applied in times such as those in which we are now living. But it will be realised one day that this simply is not possible, that the highest truths cannot be communicated when storms are raging. As far as my theme is concerned, I will give a course of lectures on it later on, when karma permits, in substitution for what was to have been given in Munich. But in view of the desire to hear something about this subject, I will try to meet this wish as far as is possible at the present time.

The essential findings of Spiritual Science are acquired through *occult reading* and *occult hearing*. We hear something about the methods by which the spiritual investigator reaches his experiences, when he speaks of the actual processes of

* It had been Dr. Steiner's intention to give a course of lectures on the theme 'Occult Reading and Occult Hearing' in August, 1914, after the production of a new Mystery Play, but this was prevented by the outbreak of the War.

occult reading and occult hearing. Absurd theories still prevail at the present time about the way in which results are obtained in Spiritual Science. Before I pass on to the central theme I will speak of a trivial matter—trivial, that is to say, in comparison with what our stream of spiritual life would like to attain. A certain modern Professor wrote a review of my book *Theosophy*. This review was published a few years ago, and the author was obviously irritated most of all by what is said in the book about the human aura, about thought-forms and so forth. Among many things that I will not mention here, this review also contains something that is absolutely comprehensible from the point of view of a typical thinker of the present day. It is said that if there is anything in these statements about the aura and thought-forms, some of those who can see thought-forms should subject themselves to an experiment. There would have to be an experiment where a number of those who claim to be able to see such things stand in front of others who have certain thoughts and feelings, and then the former should be asked: 'What do you see in these people standing or sitting in front of you?' Then—according to the reviewer—these so-called occultists should state what they have observed and the others should confirm that they had actually had these thoughts and feelings. If the seers' statements all tallied with each other, then they could be believed.

Let me say here that there is nothing more natural than this argument. Any thinker schooled in modern natural science must use it because it inevitably appears to be completely reasonable. Nevertheless, one thing holds good. The Professor who said this had certainly read the book before writing his review. We must assume this at any rate. As the review gives the impression of honesty, we can certainly assume it. But he could not read it in the real sense because, comprehensible as it is that the objections should be made as long as there is no knowledge of the truths contained in the book, it ought also to be comprehensible that such objections would not be brought forward if the book had been read with understanding. With these words I am saying something that will be considered outrageous by every normal scientific thinker of to-day—he will think it outrageous because it must inevitably be incomprehensible to him; he simply cannot understand it. Among the things to be found in that book, there is also the following.——It is said that if the seer really desires to look into the spiritual world and see the truth, he must, above all, practise a self-education which enables him to penetrate into things with absolute selflessness, to silence his own wishes and desires in face of the spiritual world. Yes, but if five or six people are brought together in order to make an experiment according to the methods of natural science, as is demanded, those four or five people start off with the wish to reach a certain result—as a matter of fact a result that is demanded by science itself. The whole thing is arranged as happens when there are desires and wishes in ordinary life—which is just what should be avoided. It is obvious that every true impression of the spiritual world will be eliminated by such an experiment. For this experiment is arranged entirely according to the thinking of the physical plane and it is just these thoughts of the physical plane that must be overcome, together with all the desires and wishes connected with them. It may be said that it is a question of being passive. Certainly—but such conditions cannot be arranged from the standpoint of the physical plane and with the methods of the physical plane. They must be arranged only from the standpoint of the spiritual world and with the methods of the spiritual world.

First of all, the matter in question would have to lie in the spiritual world itself, not in the brain of a curious professor. The intention would have to emanate from the spiritual world that human beings who are seers here on the physical plane should experience something of the thoughts and feelings of other human beings; through the karma of the spiritual world a handful of people would have to be brought together—brought together, *not* by a professor but as if through a nexus of destiny. Then, from the other side, the seers too would themselves have to be brought together by karma. Again, from out of the spiritual world the feelings and so forth within the individuals would have to be revealed to the various seers. If the experiment could be arranged in this way it would undoubtedly succeed.

If anyone reads my book *Theosophy* with real understanding, he will know that what I have just said is a self-evident truth of the spiritual world but that such procedures are not possible in our age. And one has, after all, to reckon with this fact.

Because the review in question showed me that people are not able to read the book with sufficient understanding to discover such a thought by themselves, in the sixth edition—the proofs of which I am now correcting—I have added what I have just told you. One of the essentials in a book that has grown out of Spiritual Science is that one not only assimilate its actual contents—that is of minimal importance—but that having read it a *change* shall have taken place in thinking and feeling; standards and judgments otherwise applied in the everyday world should have progressed. The difficulty still standing in the way of understanding books on Spiritual Science is that people read them just as they read other writings and imagine that their contents can be absorbed in the same way, whereas the truth is that something will be changed within us when we have understood a genuinely occult book. It is therefore quite understandable that genuine occult books are rejected by most human beings to-day. For what ought to take place in someone who reads such a book at the present time? He takes the book . . . and he is clever . . .

as everyone is clever to-day. He considers that he is capable of judging the contents of the book, and he is convinced at the outset that there can be no better judge of that book than himself. And now, after having read it, is he supposed to learn to judge differently? Of course he cannot do so; he is clever already and has impeccable judgment! He does not admit that there is anything to change in his power of judgment. Needless to say he will realise nothing of the basic trend and intention of the book. At most he comes to the conclusion that he has learnt nothing from its contents and that it is all so much juggling with words and concepts. It must necessarily be so if he does not constantly have in mind the basic principle of Spiritual Science which is that in any circumstance, no matter how trivial, after reading a genuine book on Spiritual Science, a different kind of perception and judgment of the world must arise.

There is one essential to be remembered if the words 'Occult Reading and Occult Hearing' are to mean anything to us. We must as it were say farewell to the ordinary kind of thinking, the ordinary judgments applied to the physical world. I have often emphasised that one must, of course, remain a reasonable human being. Although a new kind of judgment, of thinking and of feeling must be acquired for the spiritual world, healthy judgment as regards the events and beings of the physical plane must be maintained. That goes without saying. But there is something that is necessary for the higher worlds and does not hold good for the physical plane. I will start from an experience that is certainly familiar.

On the physical plane we are accustomed through our thinking, feeling and willing to relate ourselves to that plane. When we think, we create for ourselves mental pictures of the things and beings of the physical plane and the processes connected with them. Anything of which we opine that it is present in space or takes place in time, we thereby make into our own spiritual property. We learn, through our mental pictures, to know something. It is the same with feeling. We confront some object—for instance, we delight in a rose; we take the rose into our world, into our feeling, into our own soul. We make something that goes out as an impression from the rose and works upon our soul, into our own inner possession. In willing, we incorporate into the external world something that is contained in our intention. Relationships between ourselves and the external world are clearly evident when we observe our behaviour and conduct on the physical plane. Nothing we thus apply in acts of thinking, feeling and willing, nothing we do when we enter into relation with the outer world through the physical body, serves us in the remotest degree—in the form in which it is practised on the physical plane—for getting to know anything of the higher world. Whatever helps us for example, to know something about the physical world, whatever we apply in the form of feeling or thinking in order to know about the things of the physical world—this can serve only as preparation for spiritual-scientific investigation.

Let it be remembered, therefore, that in the physical world whatever we do in thinking, feeling and willing in order to have some knowledge of that world or to do something for it—all this serves only as *preparation* for knowledge of the higher worlds. Whatever we may think about something belonging to the physical world, no matter how astutely, gives us no knowledge of the higher worlds. Through thinking our soul is merely prepared, merely trained in such a way that it gradually becomes capable of penetrating into the spiritual worlds. And the same applies to willing and feeling in connection with things of the physical world. In order to be doubly clear, let me say this. A learned researcher, through his scientific methods, gets to know something belonging to the external world. When he has investigated it he is wont to say: I know this and that belonging to the external world. This kind of investigation, this kind of thinking, does not help him in the very least to penetrate into the spiritual world. His thinking and investigation are of significance only *because they exercise the powers of his soul*. The effect, as far as penetration into the spiritual worlds is concerned, is that through this thinking and investigation the soul becomes more capable of living its own life, of activating its own forces. The activities that are normally carried out in the physical world are of use for spiritual-scientific investigation only as an education of a man's own soul.

I will choose still one more comparison to make the matter clearer. Suppose someone is a carpenter; he has learnt carpentry and intends to make furniture. In his work as a carpenter he makes certain pieces of furniture and continues to do so for many years. This is his job. But something else happens as well; he becomes more skilful, his manipulations more effective; he acquires something else, inasmuch as his own organism becomes more skilful. This is a kind of supplementary achievement. It is the same with spiritual activities. If, as a botanist, I think and make great efforts for years in the sphere of botany, that is all to the good, but as well as this my mind becomes more flexible. That is also of help. I am better 'drilled' than I was some decades ago. Please do not take the expression in its ordinary trivial sense, if I say that the spiritual scientist must have been previously 'drilled'. He must use his drilling to make his spiritual powers more mobile, more flexible. Then, when everything that is otherwise practised in the world is placed directly in the service of self-education—as happens in meditation and concentration, in the exercises that are given for the purpose of penetrating into the spiritual world—we duly prepare ourselves for this. Please take the words, 'we prepare ourselves', as something infinitely important, for in reality we can never do anything more than *prepare ourselves* to enter the spiritual world; the rest is an affair of that world itself; the spiritual world must then come to us. It will not do so if we remain in the usual state of human beings on the physical plane. Only when we have *transformed* our soul-forces in the way indicated can we hope that the spiritual world will come to us. It cannot be anything like investigation in the physical world, for then we go towards the things we are investigating. We can only prepare so that when the spiritual world comes towards us, it will not escape us, but make a real impression upon us.

It must therefore be said: All that we can do to develop the capacity for spiritual investigation is to prepare ourselves worthily, in order that when karma wills that the spiritual world shall confront us, we shall not be blind and deaf to it. We *can* so prepare ourselves, but the manifestation of the spiritual world is an act of grace by that world, and must be thought of as such.

And so to the question: How can one succeed in penetrating into the spiritual world?—the answer must be: We must prepare ourselves by adopting every measure that makes our actions more skilful, more mobile, that trains our thinking, makes our feeling and perception more delicate, more full of devotion. And then: Wait, Wait, Wait! That is the golden rule—to be able to wait in restfulness of soul. The spiritual world does not allow itself to become accessible in any other way than this: individuals must make themselves worthy of it and then develop a mood of expectation in restfulness of soul. That is the essential. We acquire it in the way I have described in detail in my books, by making ourselves ready to receive the spiritual world. But we must also acquire that absolute restfulness of soul which alone makes it possible for the spiritual world to approach us.

In lectures I have used the following example. In the physical world, if we want to see something we must go to it.

LECTURE I

Those who want to see Rome must go to Rome. That is quite natural in the physical world, for Rome will not come to them. In the spiritual world it is just the reverse. We can do nothing except prepare ourselves through the methods described, in order to be worthy to receive the spiritual world: we must acquire restfulness of soul, poise where we stand . . . then the spiritual world comes to us. We must wait for it in restfulness of soul—that is the essential. And this that comes to us, where is it? Of this too I have often spoken and will speak of it merely by way of introduction so that we may have a good foundation upon which to proceed.

You are all familiar with our anthroposophical literature. Where are the Elemental Beings, where are the Beings of the higher Hierarchies? They are here, everywhere—just where the table is, where the chairs are, where you yourselves are— they are around us everywhere. But in comparison with the things and processes of the external world they are so ethereal, so fleeting, that they escape the attention of men. Men pass unceasingly through the whole spiritual world and do not see it because through their constitution they are still unprepared for it. If you were able to enter the spiritual world, as is the case at night when you are asleep, you would realise that consciousness is so weak that in spite of the fact that man is in the spiritual world from the time he goes to sleep until he wakes, his consciousness is too dull to perceive the spiritual Beings who are around him. He is in the spiritual world the whole night long, he is within this delicate, fluctuating world, but he is not aware of it because his consciousness is too dull.

What must happen in order that man can learn to be aware of this world in which he is really living all the time? Here we have to consider something very important. Above all, we must keep the following in mind. I have tried to describe it more precisely, for the public as well, in the last chapter of the book *Riddles of Philosophy*. I want to see whether a few individuals who are not in the Anthroposophical Movement are capable of understanding it.

How does external perception come about? As you know, people generally think—especially those who imagine themselves to be very clever—that external perception arises because the objects are there and then man, inside his skin, receives impressions from the objects; they suppose that his brain (if they think materialistically) produces inner pictures of the external objects and forms. Now that is simply not the case; the facts are quite different. The truth is that the human being is not by any means confined within his skin. If someone is looking at a bunch of flowers, then with his Ego and astral body he is actually within it, and his organism is a reflecting apparatus which reflects it back to him. In reality you extend over the horizon which you survey. In waking consciousness you are also rooted, with an essential part of your Ego and astral body, in your physical and etheric bodies. The process is as I have often described in lectures. Let us assume that here are a number of mirrors. As long as you walk through space and have no mirror, you do not see yourself, but as soon as you come to a mirror you do. The human organism is not the producer of what you experience in your soul, it is only the reflecting apparatus. The soul is united with the bunch of flowers outside. That the soul may be able to see the flowers consciously depends upon the eye, in unison with the brain-apparatus, reflecting back to the soul that with which the soul is living. Man does not perceive in the night, because when he sleeps he draws out what is within him all day—his Ego and astral body. Therefore the eyes and brain cease to reflect. Going to sleep is just as though you had a mirror in front of you—you look into the mirror and see your own face; take the mirror away, and all at once your face is no longer there!

And so man, with his being of soul-and-spirit, is actually within that part of the world which he surveys; and he sees it *consciously*, because his own organism mirrors it back to him. In the night this reflecting apparatus is not there and he sees nothing. We ourselves *are* the part of the world which we see; during the night that part of the world is withdrawn.

One of the worst forms of Maya is the belief that man remains firmly within his skin. He does not; in reality he is within the things he sees. When I am confronting a human being, I am within him with my astral body and Ego. If I were not to confront him with my organism I should not see him. The fact that I can see him is due to my organism; but with my astral body and Ego I am within him. The failure to realise this is one of the most dangerous results of Maya.

In this way we can form an idea of the nature of perception and experience on the physical plane.

And what about the spiritual world? If we want to experience that of which I have said that it is so fleeting, so mobile compared with the processes and things of the physical world that although we live within it as within the coarse objects of the physical world, we do not experience it because it is too tenuous—if we want to experience this fluctuating, ethereal reality, then our ordinary Ego, the bearer of our individuality, our egoity, must be damped down, must be suppressed. In true meditation this is what we do. What is meditation? We take some content, or mental picture, and give ourselves over entirely to it. We forget ourselves and suppress the egoity of ordinary waking consciousness. We exclude everything that is connected with the egoity of waking consciousness. Whereas we are accustomed to apply egoity on the physical plane, we now suppress it. Instead of living in the physical and etheric bodies, we gradually succeed, by suppressing egoity, in living in the astral body only.

Please note the essential point here. When we meditate or concentrate, our primary goal always is to suppress our egoity. This egoity must not transmit physical experiences; we try to suppress it, to press it into the astral body. When it is in the astral body it is not, to begin with, reflected in the physical body.

When you look at this bunch of flowers, you are, in reality, within it. The physical body is a reflecting apparatus and you see the bunch of flowers because the physical body mirrors it to you. If you suppress the Ego with its egoity, then you will be living within the astral body. And the astral body is so delicate that you can perceive the fleeting things of the external world *consciously*; but they too must first be *reflected* if you are to see them in reality.

There are many among you who faithfully and sincerely devote yourselves to meditation. Thereby you succeed in suppressing the everyday egoity, and experience in the astral body begins. But reflection must first take place if you are to have conscious experience in the astral body. There are numbers among you who through meditation have already reached the stage of living in the astral body. But now it is a matter of reflection, of mirroring. And just as in ordinary life the physical body must reflect what we experience, so, if we want to perceive consciously in the spiritual world, *the experiences of the astral body must be reflected by the etheric body.*

But what happens when a man's experiences in the astral body are actually reflected by the etheric body? Something happens of which we must realise, above all, that it is absolutely different from sight in the physical world. Things in the spiritual world are not as convenient as they are in the physical world. Even a bunch of cut flowers is a self-contained object; it remains as it is. We can take a bunch of flowers home and have pleasure in it, put it in a vase and so on. We expect nothing else when the bunch of flowers is there in front of us. But this is not by any means the case with the astral experiences that are reflected to us by the etheric body. Everything there lives and weaves; nothing is still for a single moment. But the essential thing is not how it appears in the reflection. The essential thing about the bunch of flowers is what it actually *is*, at the time. I take the flowers and I have them. When something is reflected to me by the etheric body, I cannot take it as it is and be satisfied with it. For it simply is not what it appears to be.

Understand me well, my dear friends. For this too I have often used the following analogy. Suppose there are a few strokes here (on the blackboard) let us say B . . . A . . . U. Now if I could not read when these signs are in front of me I should simply say: 'I see a few strokes like this which, when joined, form a peculiar pattern.' I cannot take this home like the bunch of flowers and put it in a vase! If I were to take what stands there, the word BAU (building) and put it in a frame, then I have not got what is essential. What is essential is the actual building outside somewhere. I express the building through these signs, and I merely *read* the essential thing, in the signs.

On the physical plane the essential things are actually there, in front of me. In ordinary reading I have not the essentials; I have signs for them. So it is with what I experience in the astral body which is then reflected in the etheric body. It is correct only if I take it as so many signs, realise that these signs mean something else and that it is not sufficient simply to look at what is reflected and assume that it is the essential thing. It is not the essential, any more than the word BAU is the actual building. The essential thing is what these signs *mean*. First of all I must learn to read them. In the same way I must learn to read what, to begin with, I perceive in the spiritual world—simply a number of signs which express the truth. We can acquire knowledge of the spiritual world only by taking what it presents to us as letters and words which we learn to read. If we do not learn this, if we think we can spare ourselves the trouble of this *occult learning to read*, it would be just as clever as a person taking a book and saying: There are fools who say that something is expressed in this book, but that is no concern of mine. I can just turn over the pages and see fascinating letters on them. Such a person simply takes what is presented to him and does not trouble about what is there expressed.

If what I have just said is ignored, one comes into an entirely false relationship to the spiritual world. The essential point is to learn to read and interpret what is perceived. We shall see in the next lectures what is meant by this reading and interpreting.

Thus we have indications at any rate, which help us to understand the question: What is occult reading? Occult reading begins when man experiences himself in the astral body—just as in the physical world he experiences himself in the Ego—and when the experiences of the astral body are reflected in the *etheric body*, not as is the case in the physical world, when the experiences of the Ego are reflected in the physical body.

Something else must be remembered here. We are not, as I have also told you to-day, wholly within the objects outside us; we are not only in them with our Ego and astral body; but in waking consciousness the Ego also sends part of itself into the physical body. It is only during sleep that the Ego withdraws from the physical body. This means that in order to live in the physical world we must be able to dive down into our physical body. As regards perception and reading in the spiritual world, we realise, in the first place, that we can live in our astral body, and that things are reflected to us by the etheric body. But we must advance to the further stage of being able to live in the etheric body itself, to come down into the etheric body just as on waking from sleep we come down into the physical body. Please take note too that it is necessary to come down with the astral body into the etheric body.

LECTURE I

When we learn to read, we learn to live outside the physical body. Just as on waking we come down into the physical body, so must the occultist, *without* sinking into the physical body, come down into the etheric body. Occultists call this, with reason, 'being thrust into the abyss'. What is necessary is that we should not be stupefied when this happens, that we should go down with consciousness and maintain our own bearings, for this descent into the etheric body is not as easy as the descent into the physical body. In very truth it is like being thrust into the abyss. Man's being is split into three. I have spoken of this in the book *Knowledge of the Higher Worlds*. Man becomes a threefold being. He cannot consciously descend into his etheric body without being multiplied in the way indicated.

When the human being lives in the physical world alone, and goes to sleep, his Ego and astral body are outside the physical and etheric bodies; his consciousness then is too dull to enable him to see the spiritual world. When he comes down into the physical body which reflects the physical world to him so that he perceives it, this too is a kind of thrust into the abyss; only it is made so easy for us that we do not experience it as a shock. But every morning, if through our exercises we progress to that stage where we can experience something in the spiritual world, if we learn to read in this condition which is like sleep that has become conscious, we also experience what it means to be thrust down, to be divided into three. If we retain our consciousness now, we are also able consciously to penetrate into the things and happenings of the spiritual world that are outside us.

Thus we learn to live in the astral body and have our experiences reflected by the etheric body. We read as when we are reading a book. As soon as we have come down into the etheric body we become threefold. We can send out these three parts of our being—and they then move about consciously in the spiritual world. In their wanderings they then experience what we call 'occult hearing'. As soon as we have been consciously thrust down into our own etheric body, *occult hearing* begins. Now we penetrate into things in the real sense. Now we notice that what we have previously learnt to read we can actually *experience*.

Let us therefore repeat what has been said. Through his occult exercises man is enabled to suppress his egoity to such an extent that he learns to live consciously in his astral body. Then, gradually, the beings and happenings of the spiritual world are reflected by his etheric body. When he is able rightly to interpret this reflected world, he has learnt the art of *occult reading*. At a further stage, when he is able not only to read while outside his etheric body, but to awaken in the real sense in the etheric body, then he sends out the three parts of his being into the world and *hears* what is going on, hears its inner weaving and activity. At this stage he *hears* it.

Gradually he develops the faculty of occult reading and occult hearing in such a way that something quite definite is associated with the experience. He succeeds in actually penetrating to the reality of things. For what transpires on the physical plane is not the reality, indeed it is not! Simple contemplation shows us in every region and corner of the world that what we experience in our environment is not the reality, that we attach a false meaning to everything. Someone once said to me on the banks of the Rhine: 'There is the ancient Rhine.' It was a beautiful, deeply felt saying. But what, in reality, is ancient in the Rhine? Certainly not the water that one sees flowing by, for the next moment it is no longer there. It shows clearly enough that it is *not* what is ancient. Ancient, at most, is the hollow that has been burrowed out in the soil, but that is not what is meant when someone speaks of 'the ancient Rhine'. What is it, in reality, that is designated by the phrase, 'the ancient Rhine'? If one says 'the hollow' . . .

well, there are hollows in the sea-floor too, and also streams. When the Gulf Stream flows through the ocean, not only is the water different at every moment but the hollow too is different. Nothing is permanent in the Physical, nothing whatever. It is the same with the whole physical world. Your own organism is only a stream: the flesh and blood you have to-day was not yours eight years ago. Nothing is real in the Physical, everything is in flow.

To speak of 'the ancient Rhine' has meaning only when we are thinking of those elemental Beings who actually have their life in the Rhine, when we are thinking of the elemental River God Rhine—a spiritual Being who is truly ancient. Only then have we said something that has meaning. We must mean the words 'ancient Rhine' in a spiritual sense, or we are talking thoughtlessly. It is profoundly true that we penetrate to spiritual realities only when we are guided by the spiritual world. It is then that we penetrate into the true realities. That we do indeed penetrate into these realities will be clear when we describe the details of occult reading and hearing—as far as is possible—in the lecture to-morrow.

LECTURE II

Identification with the Signs and Spiritual Realities of the Imaginative World

We will remind ourselves again of what I told you yesterday about the actual relationship of man to the world. I said: In reality it is Maya, illusion, to assume that as human beings of soul-and-spirit we are inside our skin, that things are merely round about us and we take their images into ourselves. In reality, as human beings of soul-and-spirit, we live in the things themselves. We could not become aware of them if our experiences were not reflected to us by our organism. Living in the ordinary physical world, the things are reflected by our physical organism, by its sensory system, by its thinking system, feeling system, willing system.

The truth, then, is this: our organism is a reflecting apparatus. What we experience is not produced in us by our physical organism—which is an erroneous conception of materialism—but it is reflected. Now just as little as a mirror produces what is seen in it, does our organism produce what we experience in our life of soul about the things around us. And the materialist who asserts that the brain or some other organ produces the experiences in our life of soul, is stating, in regard to these things, the same as one who declares that the face he sees when looking in a mirror, belongs not to him but has been produced by the mirror.

The truth of the matter, therefore, has to be experienced when we progress, in the way described yesterday, to the stage

LECTURE II

of occult reading. After due preparation we experience the more fleeting, more fluctuating beings and happenings of the spiritual world—more fleeting and fluctuating by comparison, of course, with the physical world. We see them inasmuch as we experience them in our astral body and they are mirrored by our etheric body. And we experience these reflections as pictures.

I said yesterday that, generally speaking, we can regard these pictures merely as *signs* of the spiritual reality. I made this clear by pointing out that anyone who experienced these pictures as dream-pictures (although they are far more living than ordinary dream pictures) would be subject to error. To regard these dream pictures as reality would be like someone who regarded the word BAU (building) not merely as the sign of the building but as the reality itself. We have to envisage that when those fleeting, fluctuating pictures of the spiritual world are reflected from outside by our etheric body, we have the world before us like an open book, like a book which has been opened for us but which we must first learn to read in the right way. In general terms, this is correct. But there is one principle which applies to experiences of the higher worlds far, far more strongly than to those of the physical plane: it is the principle that there are exceptions to everything, real exceptions. Especially are there exceptions to those things of which I have been speaking. This must be realised. What I have said holds good in general and if we pay heed to it we can find our bearings in the spiritual world. But there are exceptions and I will explain more concretely the extent to which this is so.

I will take a definite case. Let us suppose that somebody who has developed certain genuine clairvoyant powers, endeavours—and this lies near to the hearts of many people—to find, in the spiritual world, one who recently or some time previously has passed through the gate of death and is now living in the spiritual world in the existence which we describe as the life between death and a new birth.

As I emphasised yesterday, such a search is dependent upon the grace of the spiritual world. It is an act of grace on the part of the spiritual world to be able actually to behold the dead whom we are seeking. As a rule in such striving, curiosity will certainly not be satisfied. Anyone who were to start merely with the intention of satisfying his curiosity in searching for someone who is dead, would either see nothing at all or inevitably be exposed to errors of every possible kind.

But now we will assume that this is not the case, that there is an important reason, recognised by the Beings of the spiritual world, for meeting the dead. Let us assume that everything is in order—to use a trivial expression—and that a meeting with the dead is permissible. Here again I speak quite generally. It will not be a simple matter of the clairvoyant concerned transporting himself through meditation into the spiritual world and there directing his desires, his wishes or his thoughts to the dead in order to have the grace of vision bestowed upon him. To embark on such an undertaking presuming in advance that it will succeed, would be an error. For as a rule, something quite different will happen.

Please realise that one can only describe special cases; it is not possible to give general, abstract theories when one is speaking, as I am doing now, of a theme like this which concerns the occult world. I can only give an example.

Let us therefore assume that a seer has a justified reason for coming into contact with someone who is dead and through meditation, through concentration of his thoughts finds measures which enable this contact to take place. To describe the character of these measures would lead us too far today, but let us assume that they are right. If through meditation and concentration the soul is really in the condition in which the dead can be perceived, the seer may possibly, to begin with—if he has not already had experiences in this sphere—be very easily inclined to see something that he does not connect at all with the manifestation of the dead or with anything to do with him. He may see before him a widespread *world of pictures*, pictures that are far more living than those of ordinary dreams. Again and again I must emphasise, because so many errors are current in this respect, that this world of pictures is a world of signs, signs of the higher world. It is this world of signs that we learn to understand. We experience inwardly mobile pictures, all kinds of happenings that are connected with this or that personality. This is experienced—only to begin with there is hardly any resemblance to be found between what we are seeking and the pictures that are experienced. But one thing reveals itself when we are not on the wrong track: within this moving world of pictures we shall experience something that seems to be the most essential point. In the case of the other pictures, you will say to yourselves: these pictures contain something that reminds you of all kinds of things which might also arise from your own memory. Although you have no remembrance of these actual events, nevertheless it is possible—because they are connected with what you have experienced—for them to have given rise to remembrances that are interwoven with fantasy. It is precisely now that the genuine clairvoyant must be on the alert and remember that he is here concerned with a world of pictures which *might* have been gathered together from his memories. But there is some one point which no memory presents. You can therefore make a precise distinction between what might possibly be the result of fantasy in connection with memories and the other element that is there on its own, and around which everything else groups itself. Of that one point you know that it is *not* a memory, that it could never have come in a dream into your field of vision. Certainly one must have had a certain practice in distinguishing dream-pictures from reality before this difference can be seen quite precisely. But then the point comes where one knows: There *is* something there.

I will try to speak quite precisely. As a rule, this one thing among the pictures may, in a sense, seem even to be paradoxical, absurd. It is possible for something strange and very curious to appear in a sequence of pictures which may otherwise be so beautiful, so splendid, so powerful. The seer will very often find that this experience passes away from him again, that he really cannot begin to make anything of it. Then, of course, he must make the attempt over and over again, from the start. After he has had certain practice in seership, he will find as a rule that again and again such a sequence of pictures comes before him, pictures perhaps of a quite different kind, but there will always be among them something that is certainly the same as what previously constituted the central point of the series of pictures.

Now a certain stage of seership must have been attained if one is to succeed at the first or second attempt in doing the right things with these pictures. When the pictures are in front of us, we must *grasp* them, be completely *conscious* so that they do not fade away like dream-pictures. We must face them just as we face a thing in the external world, when we have it in our hand and can say: 'I am *here* and you are *there*.' We must be able to distinguish ourselves from the picture and must not be absorbed by it.

In order to achieve this, it is good to try deliberately to *change* something in the picture as it stands before one. Let us suppose that the picture is there in front of us and we have a conscious hold of ourselves, being able to distinguish ourselves from the picture . . . let us suppose that some personality comes into the pictures and looks at us with a frowning, unfriendly expression. And now try, while remaining in the whole situation and without freeing ourselves from the clairvoyant vision, now try to feel: How would it be if I were really kind to this person, so that he no longer looks at me frowningly, but with friendliness? If something then changes in the world of pictures it is at once easier to maintain our position within it.

The next stage must be this . . . it is difficult to find the right words because the affairs of the spiritual world are so different from those of the physical world. . . . The next stage is that we must identify ourselves with the picture, with all the pictures, sink down into them, *become one with them*. For by becoming one with them we put an important truth into execution, as we shall see. If I may use another trivial expression here—we have to consume this whole series of pictures spiritually, devour them, take them into ourselves, identify ourselves with them, sink into them. In other words, we must realise and *know*: I have now distinguished myself from these pictures, I have maintained my position outside them, and now, by my own will, I sink into them, just as if I were jumping into water in order to swim in it.—And now comes the important experience—for now you experience in your own soul everything that is expressed in this series of pictures, as if one person were fighting or wounding another or being kind to him. The experience, therefore, is: 'I am the wounder, also the one who is wounded. I am everything that is in this picture.' It is as if you had a picture before you, let us say, of someone who is being beheaded and you experience yourself simultaneously as the one who is doing the beheading and the one who is being beheaded. It is in this real way that you experience yourself in this whole fluctuating world of pictures. You yourself are every picture, every movement in it. Then the picture as such, as an Imagination, becomes invisible, but the *inner experiences* as such become all the more full of meaning. You cease, now, to behold the picture, but you live in a world of rich experience.

When we really succeed in living right in the pictures, the second act begins. But it need by no means follow immediately.

From this point onwards a great deal of discouragement may be in store for seership. It may quite well happen that the moment comes when the resolve is made to sink down into the pictures, to swim in them, and lo! they have vanished like a dream or like something that is forgotten. It *may* happen—but it will be in the rarest of cases—that the experience of which I shall now speak, comes immediately. But most often of all, what will happen is that the whole episode seems to have entirely vanished, like a dream. Now as genuine clairvoyants we must realise that it need not necessarily be a fact that it has gone altogether. The second experience—which, as I have said, follows in the rarest of cases immediately upon the first—may come much later, may come right out from among the day or night experiences. For very often, what we have thus consumed takes time to be *wholly* united with us, to be wholly 'digested', by the soul. It may take a long time. . . . But when we are sufficiently united with the experience, when it is sufficiently digested, the moment comes when we know: Now I am connected with the personality, or rather with the individuality of the dead and he is sending *his* thoughts into me. Now I am thinking what the dead is experiencing in his soul. That is what *I* am thinking now. I am connected with him; he is now speaking to me and I am listening to him.

In reality it is the picture with which we have united ourselves or the series of pictures we have taken into ourselves which has now become one with us—it is this that really hears and takes in the truth. As a rule this hearing, this spiritual hearing is no longer bound up with pictures but is borne by the consciousness that the soul of the seer is connected with the dead, and is enabling the dead to say to him things that cannot be heard by the physical ear, nor perceived with physical sight but are received together with the thoughts. Then the seer knows: This is not *thy* thought; it is what the dead is saying to thee.—

As you can realise, a certain preparation is necessary to come near an individual who has passed through the gate of death—a preparation which can be described as I have just done. Then, when we have reached this stage of hearing the dead, after having identified ourselves with the picture, all possibility of delusion is eliminated. For delusion could only be like a delusion on the physical plane if I were to meet a human being and take him to be somebody else. That, as a rule, will not occur; a human being is recognised on the physical plane. When I meet a Mr. X on the physical plane, I need not prove to myself on the basis of theoretical principles: 'That is Mr. X.' The being himself whom I meet enables me to recognise him. As soon as we stand before a being of the spiritual world, we know that we are in his presence ... although in the spiritual world he naturally speaks to us in a spiritual way, communicating something to us in a spiritual way.

What I have just described to you denotes the transition from the signs with so many meanings which we read and do not attempt to interpret with the intellect, but by absorbing, become one with them. We 'consume' them, as it were. Through the process which is set going in the soul as the result of having become one with the pictures, we prepare ourselves to *hear* the objective process, the objective reality.

The reading is a truly living process—one's very soul has to be directed to it. Something quite different is demanded than is ever demanded on the physical plane. Suppose someone were to publish a book on the physical plane and were to demand that in order to understand the book, we must first eat it, consume it ... Then suppose we were so organised that we could digest an 'A' in a different way from an 'I' and, through the inner process, realise the difference. If we could experience all this, then the process would be comparable with the spiritual process just described.

We cannot approach a spiritual happening or a spiritual being until we have given up our whole soul to understanding the happening or being concerned. We must ourselves have become one with the signs or letters of the spiritual world. We must read—and then, while we are reading, we must *hear*, spiritually.

I have said that this holds good as a general principle. But in Spiritual Science we must speak quite accurately. I say, 'as a general principle', for there are also exceptions. For instance, it may happen that some seer, when in a clairvoyant state, does not only experience a series of pictures as I have described, but actually experiences as a picture, as an Imagination, something that resembles the dead as he was in life, as an external figure. Then, of course, the seer may think that he is confronting the dead. But he can never be quite sure. It may be so, but it need not necessarily be absolutely certain. In order to explain this case, let me again make a comparison. Our ordinary script, printed script or writing script, consists of signs. If I write the word BAU (building), this word in itself has no resemblance whatever to a building. But it was not always so in the evolution of writing. If we go back to olden times we find a picture-script. Men drew pictures which still had a resemblance to what they were meant to represent. And it was out of this pictorial script that our script, consisting of signs or letters, evolved.

It is the same with the clairvoyance which may arise as the result of development by our Rosicrucian methods or the atavistic, more or less primitive clairvoyance which may arise as the result of certain conditions.

Just as our modern script of signs and letters is something

that has developed and the pictorial script is more primitive, so the clairvoyance which immediately sees what is being looked for, is a more primitive form. It is precisely *developed* clairvoyance that often will not immediately be able to see what is there to be seen. With developed clairvoyance things will be as I have described. But there are also exceptions, as for example a man may have the powers, without having trained his clairvoyance, simply from the nature of his organism. In the pictures which come to a natural clairvoyant there may be far more similarity with the spiritual happenings than there is in the pictures which come to the trained clairvoyant who has to go through the whole procedure I have described. Naturally, however, primitive clairvoyance can never succeed in reaching true Imaginations, can never learn anything with certainty. And even when things are known with certainty, they are only happenings which are connected with earthly life.

I will give you an example. Suppose someone has died and before his death put a Will somewhere, without being able to tell anyone where it is. He dies. Some person endowed with primitive, untrained clairvoyance may, in a kind of trancelike, imaginative condition, come into connection with the dead man. This person can be led by the dead so that he can actually discover the place where the Will was placed. The clairvoyant in question may even be able to show the place, the cupboard, for example, where it lies. Such things may happen but these cases are always connected with the physical plane and with something that has happened on the physical plane. They may be very complicated but they are always connected in some way with the physical life.

One will not come much further than this in the sphere of primitive clairvoyance. To move about with absolute clarity and certainty in the spiritual world the preparations of which I have spoken are necessary.

In order that in the following lectures we may get down to details of spiritual reading and hearing, I must still say something more precise about what I have told you.

I said that what lies behind the Maya of external experience becomes a truth the moment we enter the spiritual world in the way described. It is not enough to see a picture through clairvoyance and just to see pictures as we see beings on the physical plane. That is not enough. We must be able to plunge right into the pictures, we must make it come true that we *are in* the spiritual world. We do this by submerging ourselves in the pictures. We put ourselves *consciously* into a condition in which we also are under other circumstances, but without knowing anything about it. If, therefore, I have this series of pictures, with what I have described as the centre-point of them, I must go right into them, I must consume them, must be within them.

What I have described is a spiritual experience and what matters about a spiritual experience is that we understand it. To understand it we must be able to practise spiritual self-observation. During the process of submerging ourselves in the pictures, something happens that we feel—we feel it in ourselves. Just think . . . I have told you that we become conscious of our own position—separate from the Imagination . . . and then we sink into the pictures. When we are still consciously standing before them, the feeling is different from what it is when we have sunk down into them. I must try to describe these two feelings.

The moment we have sunk down into them, knowing that now we have made these pictures disappear by identifying ourselves with them, in that moment we are seized with the feeling of insufficiency concerning ourselves. These things are difficult to describe. The feeling is this: 'I am now only a *part* of what I was before—only one part.'

LECTURE II

Naturally, such observations must be made again and again before we are able to interpret these things rightly.

Again a comparison is best. It is just as though one had a 12 kilos weight, and then, without anything happening, the 12 kilos weight suddenly became only a 1 kilo weight. The feeling is: 'You are only one-twelfth of yourself and the other eleven-twelfths are outside in the universe.' It can be expressed in a diagram. One feels oneself somewhere out in the Universe, but with one's whole being. One feels: 'Out there in the Universe are still eleven-twelfths of me; my being is distributed.' It can be expressed by saying: 'I myself am at some point in a circumference and the other eleven-twelfths are distributed around that circumference. Here am I, at the point A1 and there are the other eleven-twelfths.'

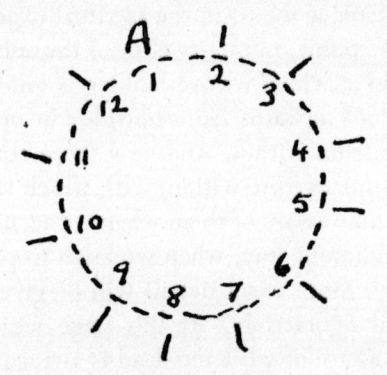

At this stage we realise that we are actually within the Universe; we have become one-twelfth part of ourselves. We have left the other eleven-twelfths of our being in a circumference.

The occult expression can be used here. We can say: Man becomes a living Zodiac. Man has himself become the Zodiac. Then comes the *hearing*; it comes from within that Zodiac. So, if I keep my former example, that of speaking with one who is dead, the dead is speaking from within the Zodiac.

OCCULT READING AND OCCULT HEARING

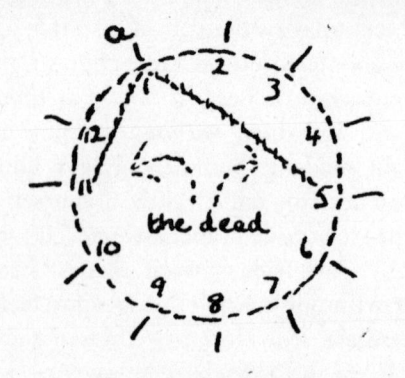

Just think of the difference between this and an experience in the physical world. In the physical world we feel enclosed within our skin; objects are outside and they seem to come into us as we look at them. In the spiritual experience we are outside at some point, in one-twelfth of the spiritual horizon. Now the world at which we are looking is *within* our circumference. We look inwards from outside; in ordinary life we look outwards from within. And now there come what seem to be spiritual voices from within, with which the dead speaks to us—we become aware of them when we accustom ourselves to listen in a different way, when we learn to pay attention in a different way. More exact details will be given—I will now just indicate it figuratively. At this stage we may have the feeling: 'I am aware of what the dead is saying; he is speaking within the circumference . . . I hear him only when my spiritual ear is turned for instance, to the 5 (see diagram). Now he ceases to speak there . . . but he goes on again, and now I only hear him when I turn my spiritual ear to another point (11) and so on.' Knowledge comes gradually when seven voices, seven different voices are distinguished within the circumference. Seven voices have to be distinguished. They are heard in the most diverse ways, according to the point from which they are heard. Everything that we experience here speaks from within the circumference, as it were from seven voices.

We have now gone out into the circumference of the Universe . . . whatever we are to experience is within this circumference. We must learn to feel ourselves as one part of that circumference and with a kind of cosmic humility, shall I say, make no claim to be anything more than one-twelfth of the circumference. But the other eleven-twelfths have to be called to our aid. We must endeavour to acquire the faculty of distinguishing what speaks to us. We must differentiate in all kinds of ways what a being can say to us in this way.

Again here, only a comparison makes things clear.—What speaks to us from within this sphere can really be called: *Spiritual Vowels*. And everything that we ourselves are, everything that lives at the periphery are *Spiritual Consonants*. Consonants and vowels work together; the consonants are stationary when we have poured out our being in twelve parts into the Universe; the vowels move within it, bringing to expression what is to be voiced.

Once again I will return to our example.—I am seeking for one who is dead, trying to come into contact with him. A series of pictures appears to me and, among the pictures, something that seems paradoxical, perhaps even absurd. I realise however that this is something which could *not* have come to me from my own life of soul. Then I succeed in sinking down into the pictures, I become one with them. At this moment I stand at a definite point—A.

My being is so submerged in what is outside that I have released, as it were, one-twelfth of my being.

You must remember that language must be *precise* when occult matters are spoken of. I have told you that the series of pictures belongs to us; we have this series of pictures in ourselves; the pictures are within that one-twelfth, and everything else that cannot become one with these pictures is now distributed over the periphery. At this stage, for a short or long period, we may really be able to receive the spiritual voice, the communication of the dead. Then we hear the dead speaking from the periphery that we ourselves have formed around that with which we want to be related.

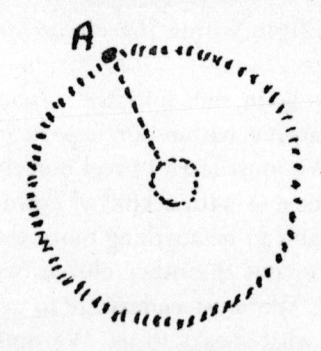

What is it that has really been done? We have gone out of ourselves, have become one with the Universe, but with only one part of the Universe. Therefore we have ourselves to become part of the Universe, to grasp with the whole of our being that of which we want to become aware. We have, as it were, built a spiritual aura around one part . . . but we cannot build it completely, we can only stand at one point; we have to build the aura out of what we, ourselves, are *not*.

Again let us repeat.—I perceive a series of pictures. To begin with I stand outside these pictures, but then I plunge into them; thereby I build a cosmic sphere around what I want to perceive; I build it with what I have given up, offered up. This cosmic sphere contains within itself—like seven planets—the *vowels* through which the dead can speak to us when we ourselves form the consonants through the twelve-foldness of our being.

We *can* only come into connection with a being of the spiritual world by enfolding him, embracing him in such a way that this very act of enfolding forms the cosmic consonants; the being can then announce himself to us in the cosmic vowels. The cosmic vowels can then act together with the cosmic consonants which we ourselves have fashioned. Then reading and hearing work together. Thus do we penetrate into a particular sphere in the spiritual world.

Now I beg you not to be led by what I have said into the error of thinking that what I have described has anything to do with the physical Zodiac or with the seven physical planets. That is not the case, and is not meant so. What happens is that in the twelve-foldness a cosmic sphere is built around the being whom we want to find. We build a world for ourselves.

Whenever, on the physical plane, we want to get to know something, we have to look at it from many different sides, from many standpoints; we have to go around it. In the spiritual world this must become a *reality*. Not only must we go around it with our whole being, we must so divide our being that we create a periphery around what we perceive. Every time there is a real spiritual perception, a spiritual periphery of this kind has been created. And only because those Divine Beings whom we have learnt to know as the higher Hierarchies have done this on a vast scale, has the Zodiac appeared.

Suppose that what I have described has been attained.— Intercourse with someone who is dead has been achieved. Suppose this intercourse could be consolidated, held static . . . then this consolidation would represent a human being—a spiritual human being, of course, divided into twelve parts, twelve fixed stars. If that which is perceived could be consolidated, a planetary system would arise. Inasmuch as the Gods did this and consolidated it into a gigantic plan, our world-system arose. Whereas we, in our single acts of clairvoyance create something transitory which naturally passes away again when the clairvoyance is over.

Our whole world-system is consolidated clairvoyance of

the Gods, of the higher Hierarchies. That is why we shall know this world only when our knowledge is based on spiritual foundations.

The physical world is something that is not at all real, it is just as little real as the water of a flowing river is real. The Spiritual alone is real. So it is too with a whole solar system. Thus we must learn to know the solar system in its reality, by deciphering it in spiritual reading and hearing. In many respects we have already done this.

LECTURE III

Inner Experiences and 'Moods' of Soul as the Vowels and Consonants of the Spiritual World

From what was said yesterday and the day before, you will have realised that occult reading and occult hearing consist in experiences of the soul. I used various comparisons to show how man must become one, firstly with the signs which reveal themselves to the seer in Imagination, and then, needless to say, with what these signs signify of spiritual realities.

I should like to begin to-day by giving you a more precise idea—as far as is possible in the few lectures that can be given, and even although it can only be an *approximately* precise idea—of what is necessary in order to advance from disordered clairvoyance to the genuine clairvoyance that may be called occult reading and occult hearing.

The first thing of which I will speak may be called the 'vowels' of the spiritual world. The way in which man learns to hear and read the 'vowels' of the spiritual world is, of course, a far, far more deeply *inward* process than any process of ordinary life. Many roundabout descriptions are necessary before we can even begin to approach what may be called the experiencing of the vowels, of the intrinsic sounds of the Cosmos. From what I indicated yesterday you will have realised that we can speak of seven such vowels—a symbolic parallelism with the planetary system.

Let us go back once again to the example I gave yesterday:

the search for someone who is dead. I took that as a starting-point and tried to describe the kind of experiences through which we gradually grow into the knowledge of the spiritual world. We heard that through the different forms of preparation which the seer has to undergo, he sees, first of all, a series of pictures, and he faces them just as he faces the things of the external world. We face a dream picture, too, just as we face the things of the external world. Only gradually do we learn to identify ourselves with the pictures, to consume them, as it were, to become one with these pictures, to live entirely in them.

But it must be clearly borne in mind that when these pictures finally lead us to find the dead or some other event or being in the spiritual world, they are signs of spiritual realities. As pictures they are realities in themselves; they express spiritual realities.

They are there, these pictures. And now the question must arise: Are these pictures only there when the seer has prepared himself in the right way and is actually able to behold them?

These pictures are not only there under such conditions. And it is very important to keep this in mind. Let us assume that you are sitting or standing somewhere and are sufficiently prepared to be able to see something. A series of fluctuating pictures appears before you. Now suppose that, instead of a seer there is an ordinary person who has no gift of clairvoyance and sees nothing of such pictures but only the pictures of the physical world. Are the pictures not there at all?— They are always there.

Let me put it as I did the day before yesterday. In reality, we are within the bunch of flowers in front of us; our perception of it depends upon its being reflected through our own organism. The moment the trained seer has a spiritual Imagination, he too is within it. In the subsequent procedure—of identifying himself with the pictures—he is simply enacting a process of consciousness; actually he is within the pictures. Nor does this apply only to a seer; even when a man confronts an object with ordinary physical eyes and ordinary mental activity, not only is he within the physical object—which, as we have seen, is in itself merely an illusion—but he is within the Spiritual. He is always within the spiritual Beings who are not physically incarnate. He is really all the time within those spiritual pictures of which the clairvoyant sees a part. They are always in the environment and we are always within them. They remain imperceptible, invisible, because man's faculty of perception is too dull, too coarse to perceive these delicately weaving beings and formations with the ordinary senses.

But this is speaking in the abstract. We could also ask: All that weaves spiritually around the world—in which we ourselves *are*—why is it that we do not become aware of it? Why is this?

We begin for the first time to understand why this is so when we have identified ourselves with Imagination, when we actually carry out the process I described yesterday. We really understand, then, why the human being cannot be conscious in the spiritual world that is round about him. What is this experience?

Let us repeat once again.—A series of pictures is arrayed before the soul; we try to identify ourselves with these pictures. We know, then, through the experiences of our own soul, that we consume these pictures, as it were; we are united with these pictures. We now know that this is so.

But at this moment, too, we can answer the question as to why we have to be outside the body, why we have to go out of the body and identify ourselves with the pictures if we are to perceive them. They *can* only be reflected back from our own etheric body. When this has become an actual experience we know why it is necessary.

Through our experiences in connection with these pictures with which we have identified ourselves, we know the following.—If, having completely identified ourselves with the pictures, we were to pass back again into the physical body, if we did not remain outside the body and wait until the etheric body reflected the pictures back, then we should take back into the physical body everything with which we had become one—we should take it back into the space that is enclosed by the skin, and we should immediately destroy the physical body to the point of death. The germ of death would be in the physical body. We may not carry into the physical body that with which we have identified ourselves. This can happen only when death comes in reality. When death does really come in earthly existence, the soul has reached the point where it can identify itself with what lives in the external world as Imagination in the natural course of life. But that *is* death.

So you see, my dear friends, we may take in deep, deep earnestness the great motto which runs through all occult studies. It is the utterance made by all those who have become occultists in the true sense of the world.—The moment genuine clairvoyance is attained, the experience is that of facing death. We reach the Gate of Death.

I have often emphasised this from another side. We learn to know how it is with a human being when he passes through the Gate of Death. Clairvoyance cannot be attained without passing through this most solemn moment which is described by occultists as 'Standing before the Gate of Death'.

But we must learn something else as well. I have spoken of this from another angle in a lecture-course given at Munich.*

* The title of the lecture-course was: *On Initiation. Eternity and the Passing Moment*. (English translation available in typescript.)

LECTURE III

We learn in deepest earnestness to put a question that is a vital question of Spiritual Science. We ask: What is the truth of our existence as human beings, living as we do within the fluctuating web of spiritual Beings which we dare not carry into our physical body because that would always mean the germ of death? Outside, Imaginations are always around us, we are within a sphere of Imaginations . . . and they must not pass into us. What comes from these Imaginations into us? Shadow-pictures, reflections, mirror-mages—these come as our thoughts, our mental images. Outside, they are the real, full-blooded Imaginations. They reflect themselves in us and we experience them in the weakened, shadowy form of our thoughts and mental images. If we carried them in their full reality into ourselves and not merely had them as reflections, we should at each moment stand before the danger of death.

What does this mean? It means that the cosmic world-order guards us from experiencing, in their full reality, these spiritual Beings and happenings, which are always around us; we are protected, inasmuch as in our everyday consciousness we contact only the shadow-pictures of these spiritual Beings. And yet, a whole number of these Imaginations belong to us, belong to the forces which are creatively active in us. The creative forces that are within us live in this world of Imaginations. We may not experience them in their primal form, but only in the shadowy form in which they are within us as *thoughts*. This can only happen through someone taking away from us the experiencing of the Imaginations which belong to our thoughts.

They have, nevertheless, to be experienced! But *we* cannot experience them. They have to be experienced by Beings stronger than we are, by Beings who can endure them in their organisation of spirit-and-soul without coming to the danger of death. Whenever we are thinking, whenever we are active in our life of soul, a spiritual Being must hold sway over us all the time, depriving us of the experience of the Imaginations underlying our thoughts and mental pictures. If you have any thought, any experience in your life of soul, this experience corresponds to a world of Imaginations. And a Being must rule over you, guard and protect you, taking away from you what you yourself cannot accomplish.

Here we have reached a point where we can speak in a more real sense than hitherto, of the Beings of the next higher Hierarchy, of the *Angeloi*. They are now spiritually comprehensible. We see them there, we see how they must watch and guard what we ourselves are not capable of accomplishing.

But it can and must happen to the seer that he becomes aware with far greater distinctness of what I have just told you. And that is the case when he goes one stage further in his seership.

We spoke yesterday of what leads to identification with the series of pictures which appears before us. The Imaginations are consumed, sucked in. Thereby they disappear as pictures outside us—but we experience them within us, we have become one with them.

But the thing can go still further. I will start by describing the subjective experience. I told you yesterday something which I have repeatedly described. When one is sunk in meditation and concentration, something approaches which one is seeking—a series of pictures arises with which one can identify oneself. I said that something else can happen. When meditation and concentration have called forth these pictures and we have tried to get right into them, the occult reading and hearing, the real perception of the spiritual being of the dead does not necessarily arise. The whole process may break off just like a process in a dream and the consequences may appear only later.

But if we go further, if we have the necessary patience and endurance to make progress in occult development through meditation and concentration, then we experience the process in still another way.

It can be experienced in the following way.—We set ourself the task of observing some being or process in the spiritual world. We sink into meditation or concentration. Thereby we draw ourselves out of the physical world and pass into the condition where the meditation, that is to say, the content of the soul we ourselves have evoked, flows by and we can feel the transition. There seems to be greater darkness . . . that which the soul has evoked flows away from the pictures, and they come up again, far, far more vividly than in a dream.

Now we confront them consciously and again dive down into them. Again there may come a moment when we know: 'You have now identified yourself with the pictures, you have become one with them, you are within them.' But we no longer feel our own existence; we feel as though we have sunk into the Cosmos—nevertheless as if we were in universal nullity.

Thus we have identified ourself with the pictures, have extinguished them—and have got nothing in their place. But now, through the practice of meditation, we have succeeded in not being brought to despair by the belief that we are losing ourselves in Nothingness. We have not the feeling of being utterly forsaken that might easily arise. In short, we plunge, as though swimming in an ocean of nullity, into the Cosmos. And then it is like waking up, but not out of a sleep, out of something with much stronger reality. At the moment of waking, we know: This was not sleep! We have not passed through the emptiness of sleep. Something has happened in the interval, something at which we were present, and now we have wakened again! We have in our consciousness the happenings which we could not experience at the time with full consciousness. But afterwards we know quite definitely that we *have* experienced them. It is like a memory! We remember something we have gone through not with the ordinary self, but with what transcends the ordinary self. Now it enters our consciousness and we experience that at which we aimed, the task we set ourselves. And now, when we meditate on what has happened, we know: 'You have gone through something as a *thinking* being (only "thinking" here has a much higher significance than in the physical world). You have gone through this as a thinking being. But however highly developed you are as a human being, you cannot experience what you have now gone through.' It is something that the human being himself *cannot* experience. Therefore in the time that has transpired between the diving down and the re-emergence, another Being had to take over the function of thinking for you, and think *in you*. You cannot yourself do the thinking. You can only remember afterwards what this Being thought in you. It was an Angelos who was thinking! And we know that in that intervening period we were interwoven with our Angelos. The Angelos experienced it for us and because the Angelos experienced it, our own consciousness was suppressed. Now we waken and remember with the ordinary life of thought what the Angelos experienced in us.

That is the process. This is the way in which, as a rule, spiritual experiences are attained. We attain them in such a way that we know: We must first pass into a condition where a Being of the next higher Hierarchy enters into us, identifies himself with us. What we cannot do in our own weakness, we *can* do through a Being of the next higher Hierarchy who is within us—but our consciousness is suppressed. We cannot have the experience in its immediate reality, but we have it afterwards, in memory and in full Ego-consciousness.

And so it is that the spiritual experiences vouchsafed to us are experienced at one time but we become conscious of them at another.

LECTURE III

I spoke of an experience I had concerning our dear friend Christian Morgenstern—a real experience, needless to say. But we become conscious of such an experience *afterwards*, because a Being of the next higher Hierarchy must take over the function of knowledge during the actual experience.

Again you will understand why this must be. If we were to bring into our own organism what a Being of the higher Hierarchies experiences in us we should not only kill our organism, but we should burst it, as through an explosion, into its very atoms. If we carried down these experiences into our own organism we should not only bring about its death, but simultaneously, its cremation.

Now you see again that seership brings us into connection with what we call the Gate of Death. We can really only know what death signifies by raising ourselves to that life of soul which can come from the experiences described.*

Only thereby can we understand the human individuality when it is outside the physical body. But then we also know how it has to be received into the higher Hierarchies—in order that it shall not work as a destroying, death-bringing force to a being of the physical plane, our own being, to begin with. The feeling of the human soul resting in the bosom of a Being of the higher Hierarchies becomes real, infinitely real. Now for the first time we get to know how things appear on yonder side of death. We know: Here in our earthly life we are surrounded by minerals, plants, the animal and the human kingdoms. On yonder side of death we enter the realm of the higher Hierarchies, to whose environment we belong just as here we belong to the environment of the physical beings around us. A feeling of kinship with the Beings of the higher Hierarchies comes into our soul. Then we learn to know that true entrance into the spiritual world is simply not possible

---

* See the lecture-course entitled, *The inner Nature of Man and Life between Death and a new Birth*. (Obtainable from Rudolf Steiner Press.)

without bringing in its train feelings of piety, feelings of being given up to the higher, spiritual world. But these feelings have the nuances I have described.

This is able to evoke a necessary 'mood' of soul. I can only express it by calling it that mood of soul in which we feel ourselves resting in the spiritual worlds. We need this mood of soul for any real experience of the spiritual worlds, just as here, in the physical world, in order that we may be able to understand our fellow-man, we have to use the larynx and other organs of speech, to utter the sound EE. What makes it possible in ordinary human speech to utter the sound EE, produces, in the higher worlds, the experience that flows from devotion. This kind of devotion is one of the vowels of the higher worlds. We can perceive nothing, read nothing, hear nothing in the higher worlds unless we can hold this mood of soul—and then wait for what the Beings of the higher worlds have to impart to us because we bring to them this mood of soul.

It is out of these moods of soul, out of this attitude to the higher worlds that the vowels of the Cosmos are composed.

If there is this feeling: Around you is a world but you cannot live in it with your feeble human powers. What surrounds you while you live in your physical body can be perceived only in the shadow-pictures of your thoughts and concepts, or rather is reflected by them. You may not experience these Imaginations directly. Your Guardian Angel must take this experience away from you in your ordinary life.— When a man feels this inwardly, with the necessary timbre of inner piety, he is able to become aware of *one of the vowels of the spiritual world*.

A next stage depends upon the development of something I indicated in my book, *The Threshold of the Spiritual World*. We grow into the spiritual world as I have there described. The process is that we emerge from ourselves as it were and identify ourselves with another being. But this is not sufficient, in no way is it sufficient. It is necessary not only to be able to identify ourselves with other beings but also to be able to *transform* ourselves into other beings, so that we do not merely remain what we are, but are able to metamorphose ourselves into other beings, actually to *become* that into which we penetrate.

A good preparation for this faculty is to practise over and over again a loving interest in everything that is around us in the world. It is impossible to express how infinitely significant it is for the developing occultist to awaken this loving interest for everything in the surrounding world. This is a hint that is, unfortunately, not usually taken deeply enough, hence the lack of success that often attends occultism. It is only too natural for the necessary power of interest to be maintained only in oneself. Even if a man will not admit it, the necessary power of interest is applied only to himself. It may be given another name, but none the less there is very little *real* interest in other things, and by far the greatest for oneself.

It must of course be said that cosmic law decrees that a man must have interest in himself, and indeed it requires great effort not to be interested the whole time in himself. It is after all a natural part of life on the physical plane. I will ignore the fact that if we have some illness, pain or disorder, this interest is always there. It cannot be otherwise. In such a case, of course, efforts might make it possible for a man not to be interested in himself—but that is extremely difficult. It might happen that a man falls ill and is not specially interested in the fact that he has this illness; he may be quite indifferent to it. What *does* interest him may be how this illness has arisen out of the whole Cosmos, how at some point in the Cosmos something arose that now is within his own skin. In such a case the man is interested in a severe illness in the same way as if it were something outside himself!

You will admit that what I have described is very difficult. And so it is with most things, at least on the physical plane. It is very difficult to take the most ordinary things we experience in our senses and thoughts as if we were standing outside them as objects. But this is just what we must try to do. And because it is so difficult it is not as a rule attempted. But everyone may be sure that if with great zeal he carries out the exercises described in the book, *Knowledge of the Higher Worlds*, he will gradually attain this knowledge.

But for this we must adopt the standpoint therein described —the exercises are not practised at all adequately. The knowledge will be attained only along by-paths because it is extremely difficult. It will be attained in the same measure in which interest in our own self decreases, so that we are no longer an interesting *subject* for ourselves, but an interesting *object*. That does no harm; it is indeed very useful because we ourselves are an object which is always to hand—only it must not be confused with the subject!

Now in the same measure in which we ourselves begin to become an *object*, we begin to be interested in everything outside us, and then we develop loving interest in the world and its phenomena. When the loving devotion to the world and its phenomena develops more and more, the mood of soul is able to intensify to the point where we not only pass out of ourselves but are able to metamorphose ourselves into other beings. Gradually we become capable of this. But such things are difficult for the soul of man and all kinds of help must be sought if this loving devotion is to exist.

I will indicate something that can be a help. A beginning can be made by making the physical world a motive for a kind of occult reading. I have often given an example from which it is good to start. If we confront a human being and look at his countenance, we realise: this boundary of the skin, these lines, what the eye sees—that is not the essential, that is the physiognomical expression of the indwelling soul. And if we had a drawing of the lines—the lines would not be the essential, but the soul which has given itself these lines as its form. And then we can look at external nature around us as though it too were an outer physiognomy. Materialistic investigators face the things of external nature just as if one were to say of a human being: 'To talk of an indwelling soul is unreal, it is fantastic superstition. All that concerns me are the forms that can be measured and investigated.'

This is how ordinary men investigate external nature. But we can say to ourselves: Just as it comes naturally to see a man's countenance as the physiognomy of his soul, so we can look at the whole of external nature, not in the ordinary way but as the physiognomy of spiritual Beings behind it. And it is good here to look at the whole world of *animals* as the physiognomy of outer nature. It requires further insight and study not to see in the animals what is usually seen but to see in them something that may be conveyed in the following words.—

There is the eagle, flying towards the Sun; that is the direction upwards, into the spiritual worlds. I will take you, the eagle, as the symbol of rising into the spiritual worlds. I look at the human *brow* and see something suggesting the eagle-nature, something that is striving upwards into the spiritual worlds. I see how what is expressed in the human soul gives the physiognomy. The eagle is part of the physiognomy of external nature. In the soaring eagle I see something suggestive of the brow in the human countenance. I look at a bull and see how it is bound to the Earth as it chews its food, how it is only in its real element when it is given over entirely to the process of digestion, how in its whole life-process it is bound up with what it takes from the Earth. The bull suggests earthly gravity to me. Then I look at the human being and feel, spiritually: There too there is something of earthly gravity, but it is held in check, kept in equilibrium by the eagle nature in man. I feel how the bull nature is also in man but it does not express itself in the same way as in the bull itself. The bull nature is seen to be a physiognomical expression. So, too, is it with the lion nature when I contemplate the heart in man and compare it with the lion in external nature. In this way we can look at the whole world of the higher and lower animals.

There have been men who have related eagle, bull and lion to the human soul and they have made drawings. Such men have attempted to read what is written in the animal world and to glean from it—but in this case separated into its single letters—what is experienced as a totality in connection with the human being. Briefly, we can say: *The physiognomy of nature is the animal world*.

But it is not only the physiognomy which interests us when we contemplate the human being. When we try to go more deeply into the soul, we are interested in what we call the facial expressions. When the physiognomy is in movement, we come nearer to the soul through the play of facial expressions than through the physiognomy as such. Again in external nature we can find this play of expression of the spiritual world behind. We find it when we look at the world of plants, at its shades of colour, its budding in spring, its blossoming throughout the summer. The Earth first thrusts it out and then, from the other side, the forces of the spheres enter into it, charming forth living movements in its infinite blossoming, growing and greening. When we look at this world of plants and relate it to a spiritual reality of the Cosmos behind it just as we relate a man's facial expressions to his soul—then this again is an exercise.

Thus we can say: *The plant world is the mien of nature*. And then come *gestures*, *movements* which emanate from the soul.

Just as we can call the animal world the physiognomy of

nature, the plant world the mien of nature, so we can now see the *forms of the mineral world* as the *gestures of nature*. And to one who is practising occult reading and hearing in the real way, it is one of the most beautiful things that can happen to him to experience the mineral world in such a way that in the forms of the surface-boundaries of the minerals, in their characteristic relations to the Cosmos outside, in their irridescence, transparency, in the crystalline clarity of the quartz, of the lime-salts, of emerald and chrysoprase, he sees the infinitely diverse gestures of the spiritual Beings behind nature.

If we carry out such exercises, if we can really experience in the otherwise dead stones what is expressed through this dead mineral kingdom, and is as if a soul were expressing in living gesture what lives in it—this is a help towards acquiring loving interest for all the beings that are around us. Then we gradually reach a stage of development in which—when the attainment of seership is possible—we are also able to transform ourselves into the beings around us. We realise that we have the power to do this. We can transform ourselves into all other human beings, but practice is necessary in the way described. The human being is capable of infinite metamorphoses in this connection.

Again we can put a question, but before doing so let me speak of the *feelings* that are bound up with what I have described. The first experience brings about an attitude to the Hierarchies; the consciousness of being protected becomes a feeling that is suffused with *piety*. The feeling of being able to transform oneself into all the diverse beings brings *respect* for the *humanity* of man. We learn to value it in all its preciousness—the humanity that we do not find in the physical world, that we do not find in ourselves, but only find when we have really become another being. The feeling that necessarily accompanies the faculty of transformation does not lead us to pride, for every single transformation tells us that we are not as worthy as the being into whom we must transform ourselves. Realisation of the faculty of transformation means, at the same time, *humility*. A feeling of deep religious humility is bound up with the realisation of the faculty of transformation.

But another question can be raised. We evoke these powers of transformation from our inner being. Are they, then, within us all the time? Yes; just as the Imaginations we call up in the way described yesterday and today are always around us, so too are these powers of transformation always within us. But in order to have conscious control of them, we must develop in the way I have told you. At every moment we are not only ourselves but every other being as well. It is only that we do not develop our consciousness highly enough. We shall best understand this by thinking of the cases in life where a man on the physical plane transforms himself into another being.

On the physical plane, of course, man uses the forces which are in other circumstances the forces of transformation. But he uses them without knowing anything of them. He uses them every time he dominates his fellow-men by unjustifiably exerting his will over them, every time he does injustice to his fellow-men. This incorporates into his fellow-man something that is unjustified. He gains a certain power thereby because the lie goes on living in the other man.

So is it whenever evil is done. The forces with which some evil is done in the world are these same forces of transformation, *but in the wrong place*. Everything evil in the world is the unlawful application of these powers of transformation. Profound insight into the secret of existence arises when we know whence come the injustice, evil, crime and sin that happen in the world. They happen because the best and most holy powers which exist in man, the powers of transformation, are applied in the wrong way. There would be no evil in the world if there were not these *most holy powers of transformation*.

LECTURE III

Even in a public lecture I once indicated this mystery of the power of evil, saying that it is the distorted application of the power which, in its proper place, would lead to the highest good.* This mood in the soul which comes when we know: Here in each human soul is something which on the one side can transform itself into all beings, and on the other, into egoism ... this is the mood with which we must confront the Cosmos if it is our aim to have *spiritual hearing*. That is a second vowel.

The mood we can have in regard to the mystery of evil as I have presented it to you, is the third vowel—what we experience when we know whereby a man may become evil. If we understand the mystery that it is the highest forces that in evil are applied in a distorted way, then we have the mood of a third cosmic vowel. These moods of soul must be actually *experienced*.

Thus we have spoken of three cosmic vowels. It has taken some time to-day; we will speak of the others to-morrow. I had first to speak of the principle that is essential for establishing in inner experience that relationship to the Cosmos whereby, in dedicating our own powers of soul, we become hearers and readers of what is happening out yonder in the spiritual world.

* The title of the lecture was: *Evil in the light of Knowledge of the Spirit.* Berlin, 15th January, 1914. (Not yet available in English translation.)

LECTURE IV

Inner Mobility of Thought

Yesterday I tried to speak of certain inner experiences which can be called the 'vowels' of the spiritual world.

We heard how occult reading and occult hearing are very living inner experiences to which the whole personality, the whole soul must be dedicated. I mentioned three such experiences for which careful preparation has to be made. One of these arises when we learn gradually to enter with *consciousness* that supersensible world in which we always are, but unconsciously, and thereby reach the Gate of Death. I also spoke of the experience which comes when we acquire the so-called faculty of transforming ourselves into other beings. And then I tried to show how we can so regard *evil* in the world that we recognise its origin in a *misuse* of higher spiritual forces which in their place and in their own mode of working are entirely justified.

Another such experience comes if we take in earnest something that is linked with the last. We must transform ourselves into other beings but in such a way that the threads of inner soul-experiences are held intact. If they cannot be held intact it is just the same as when a man on the physical plane cannot remember what happened yesterday or some years ago in his physical life. Just as this continuity of experience has to be maintained in normal physical life, so the connecting thread must be maintained through the transformations in the spiritual world. This means that when a human being has transformed himself into a certain being or event he must not lose himself. He must retain a kind of higher, purely spiritual memory of other forms, processes and beings of the spiritual world. In other words: man has to become a multiple being, to 'split up' as it were in the spiritual world, to be able to divide himself. This inner experience produces a strange feeling: 'You are here, you are this being, but you are also another being. You are within separate beings.' Without this feeling of *multiplicity* we should never be able to attain a real picture, for example, of the Beings of the higher Hierarchies. Along the paths we described yesterday and along others too we can get a picture of the Angeloi, the Hierarchy immediately above us. But to reach a more spiritually adequate picture of the Archangeloi, we must understand through inner feeling something of the experience of being multiplied. For it is only gradually that we learn to understand these Beings of the Hierarchies. We only gradually learn to understand because in the physical world all human conceptions, all human thoughts are bound up with the ordinary conditions of space and time. But quite different conditions of space and time exist when we ascend to the Beings of the Hierarchy of Archangeloi.

Starting from the ordinary physical consciousness, we have a certain basic feeling which is quite natural to this physical consciousness. If, for instance, through seership, I want to approach a human being who is living between death and a new birth, then—I am not speaking of myself here but quite generally, of one who has seership and is seeking for a dead soul—I have this feeling: 'The dead is there, together with me!' So far as the time element is concerned I can seek him just as on the physical plane I can seek another human being who is a contemporary . . . it is only a matter of finding the way to him. When we are seeking one who is dead, this idea is also quite correct. In a certain sense it is still correct when it is a question of finding a Being of the Hierarchy of Angeloi. But it is no longer correct if we are seeking for a Being of the Hierarchy of Archangeloi, because such a Being has concentrated his consciousness at a time that is not our present time.

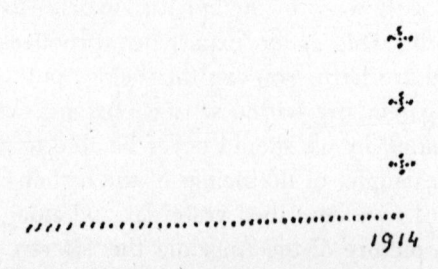

⁓⁌⁓

⁃⁌⁃

⁃⁌⁃

```
///////////////...........................
                              1914
```

Suppose this line represents the flow of time. If the seer lives at this point, 1914, and is seeking a dead soul or a Being of the rank of the Angeloi, he finds that Being somewhere in the spiritual world at the same point of time. But this does not succeed if we are trying, for instance, to find a certain Being of the Hierarchy of the Archangeloi.

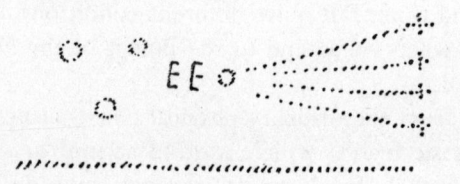

```
    ○  ○                         ....⁝
          E E ○  ············⁝
       ○                         ············⁝
///////////////////////////////////////////
```

In this case we have to transcend time, to overcome the principle of synchronism (*Gleichzeitigkeit*). In order to find a certain Archangelos we must go back, for example, to the fifteenth century. Thus we do not remain in our own epoch. Supposing this were the year 1914, we have to go back, say, to the year 1465 and seek there (EE) for the Archangelos. His influence, it is true, rays over into our own epoch but here we have merely the influence, we do not find the Archangelos in his own real identity. Other Archangeloi must

LECTURE IV

be sought for at different points (see the upper circles in the diagram). We have to go beyond time. It is a difficult conception but we have to reach it.

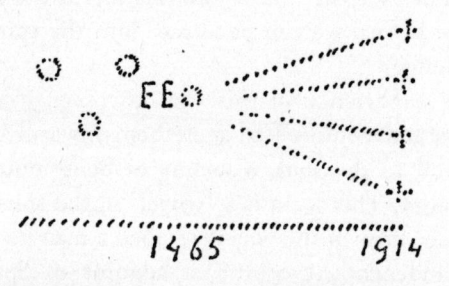

We must realise that the name '*Arch*angelos' has meaning. We know for the first time why they have this name when we find them in the way described. They are 'Angeloi of the *Beginnings*'. They are always to be found at the beginnings of epochs of time on the stage of world-history. It is there that we find them in their full consciousness, in their real self; this remains through the following epochs in the influences streaming into the flow of time. To find the Archangeloi we must not remain in the present; we must go out of time and seek for the beginnings of epochs. Thus nobody whose soul is only able to live, let us say, in October 1914, is in a position to find all the Archangeloi—perhaps not even one. This is possible only to one who can transfer his soul back into other epochs, in such a way that he can actually experience those other epochs, live in those other epochs.

But then it is necessary not to forget how we got there—just as in the physical world we must not forget what we did yesterday. This is a law of the multiplicity, of the *outpouring into number*.

And as regards the Primal Beginnings, the Spirits of Personality, the Archai, we find them only by going back to the middle of the Lemurian epoch, when the Earth was at the beginning of its physical evolution. There we find the Archai in their essential nature. We cannot find the Archai if we remain in the present.

Thus you can see that the whole relation of the soul to time must change before we can penetrate into the spiritual world with knowledge.

What we experience in this way—or even if we envisage these things and continue to feel them inwardly—imparts a kind of mood to the soul, a feeling of being outpoured into spiritual reality. This again is a 'vowel' in the spiritual world.

You can see how in the way described a man becomes more and more independent of the standpoint of Space, of the standpoint of Time, which are his in the physical world. He does not only go out of himself, but also *into* something: into the living weaving and working of the Cosmos, not only one-pointedly, inasmuch as he experiences himself in the spheres of Space, but many-sidedly, inasmuch as he experiences himself in Time as a living being, having in himself the centres of consciousness of the Beings of the higher Hierarchies. When, therefore, a man no longer lives only in himself, no longer even in the Space and Time known to him as a physical being, but when he has 'taken Space to his body' and 'Time to his soul'—mark this well, for its full meaning only dawns upon us gradually—when he has taken Space to his body and Time to his soul, he then experiences something that is not an abstract feeling in spiritual generality, but a living weaving and working in a cosmic existence full of meaning. Everywhere there is *meaning*; it pours into his soul. *Universal* meaning, weaving and living in the Universe forms itself out of individual meaning. The meaning of things bursts forth like fruit out of many centres. And the Spiritual bursting forth in the single individual meanings weaves itself into a Cosmic Word that is full of meaning. Man lives and weaves within the Cosmic Word. This experience again is another vowel of the spiritual world—the original, primal vowel of the spiritual world. This *experiencing of the Cosmic Word* which must be pictured in its living wealth and not merely as a spiritual hearing, is *Inspiration* in the higher sense. With this Inspiration we can say: 'What I know in this Cosmic Word, the Cosmic Word *knows in me.* It is not I who know, but the Cosmos knows in me. I fall short in knowledge of the Cosmic Word only because I am an imperfect instrument which can only let the Cosmic Word sound into me in broken streams. But it is the Cosmic Word itself which sounds in me.'

Humility increases the more we succeed in surrendering ourselves selflessly, without any pretentiousness in regard to our own achievement, our thinking, feeling and willing. The more we succeed in letting the Cosmic Word hold sway in the weaving of our own being, the more objectively do we reproduce, through the Cosmic Word, the mysteries pervading the universe.

Thus again we have spoken of a cosmic vowel. As I can tell you only the essential principles, I wanted to give you an idea—although quite a primitive one—of what may be called the 'vowels' of cosmic Being.

When a man is inwardly schooled in such feelings as I have described them in these five cosmic vowels, when he can experience what *can* be experienced in the life of soul as an echo of these feelings, then the soul can listen to what is going on in the spiritual world and is there in the spiritual world. And then the spiritual world can speak to the soul.

What is it that happens when real communion with the spiritual world is cultivated in the way described? Ego and astral body—but the Ego has reached a higher stage because it has become selfless and has been submerged in the astral body —Ego and astral body are outside the physical and etheric bodies. With his Ego and astral body man is outside the physical and etheric bodies when, during life between birth and death, he is engaged in acts of spiritual perception; but he look back to the etheric body and it is the etheric body that reflects these 'vowels'.

The etheric body has the power of a seven-fold reflection. I have spoken of five of these reflections. There are still two other experiences of which we could speak if it were possible to go into greater detail. But the characteristic weaving and working of the etheric body, what it reflects in its life-processes, may be described as these 'vowels'. In other words: something happens in the etheric body when a man has developed the feelings connected with the experience of standing at the Gate of Death, or is able to face Evil with understanding, or when he lives in the Cosmic Word. According to the particular mood with which he confronts the spiritual world, something is reflected in the etheric body which he is then able to perceive. It is very difficult to describe these things. Cosmic Being reflects itself in a seven-fold way in the etheric body. Let me make a diagram.—If

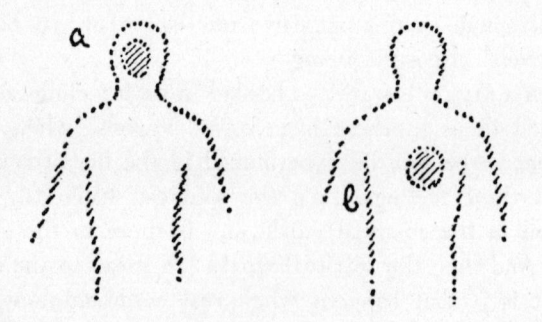

this represents man's etheric body (quite diagrammatically) —then, if a man confronts the spiritual world with the feeling that arises from the preparation for standing at the Gate of Death, his etheric body is as it were compressed up to here, at *a*, and acquires a certain radiance and resonance. And out of this radiance and resonance proceeds something that may be called one of the vowels of the spiritual world.

If a different mood is developed, the etheric body concentrates in another region—let us say, in the region of the heart (*b*). A different radiance and resonance are perceived, as emanating from the being into whom the Ego and astral body have been transposed.

What I have said up to now has referred to the 'vowels' of the spiritual world. But there are also *'consonants'* of the spiritual world, twelve consonants. We get at these consonants most easily by taking the physical body in the same way as we have taken the etheric body with its 'vowels'. The physical body is then revealed in its *twelvefoldness*.

There is not sufficient time even to hint how we can experience the twelvefoldness of the physical body as we have experienced the sevenfoldness of the etheric body. But this I must say: To a man who is conscious outside his physical and etheric bodies, they become something quite different from what they are when he is living in them. The etheric body, then, is what contains the life-process which makes us living beings. The physical body is that which builds up the organism of our senses. We are within and we use our physical and etheric bodies to make us the beings we are on the physical plane. But when, in the sense indicated, we are outside the physical and etheric bodies, they appear to us as *signs*. True, the etheric body is still composed of life; but its task, that of being the life-principle of our physical organism, does not now reveal itself. The etheric body reveals itself as the signs of the seven vowels. It becomes objective, something at which we look and which in its variability and mobility becomes the 'vowels' of the Cosmic All. We become as foreign to our etheric body as to the vowels of physical script. And we become as foreign to the physical body—which is now revealed as a totality of twelve consonants brought together—

as we are to the consonants of ordinary script. And just as consonants and vowels interpenetrate in the words of ordinary script, enabling us to read or hear, so in the spiritual world do we hear or read the etheric body which reveals itself in a sevenfold aspect by being joined with two or with three consonants of the physical body. On the physical plane, when we meet a human being we can understand him because he speaks to us, perhaps also by gesture or facial expression—but we must have eyes to see and ears to let the word enter our soul. Just as everything that constitutes a relationship to other human beings is transmitted by way of the senses, a similar thing happens in the spiritual world.

We prepare ourselves, let us say, to find a human soul who is living between death and a new birth. We know through inner experience that we are now united with that soul, that we are having experiences with it at the same time and in the same place in the spiritual world. Just as in the physical world we have sense-organs in order to come to terms with other human beings, so in the spiritual world we have to look back to the etheric body and the physical body. And in their interplay they reflect how the single processes of the etheric body are joined with those of the physical body—vowel processes with consonant processes. This interplay expresses the speech that is going on with the soul of the dead and is therefore necessary for understanding that soul.

Try to picture the following.—In the spiritual world you are united with the soul of one who is dead and is living between death and a new birth. You look back on your physical form which you can observe because you lived or are living in it on the physical plane; you also look back on the etheric form, and this reflects back all that you speak with the dead, what he has to communicate to you, what he is thinking, feeling and willing. The etheric and physical bodies have become one collective *sense-organ*. And we can say: In our

LECTURE IV

physical life we have received the physical and etheric bodies so that we may have sense-organs for the spiritual world. A new light is now thrown on the truth that life in the physical world is not merely life in a vale of sorrow of which we must long to get rid, as false asceticism teaches. We realise that life in the physical world has its sublime, divine mission. Within the physical world we acquire what becomes sense-organs for the spiritual world.

You will understand this still more precisely if I tell you about the perception of spiritual beings and happenings when we ourselves are living between death and a new birth, that is to say, when we are not seeing the spiritual world clairvoyantly from the physical plane but are united in the spiritual world with spiritual beings. As long as we bear a physical and an etheric body as a garment, so long have we instruments for reflecting; these bodies serve us as sense-organs. When we lay aside these bodies at death, we naturally no longer have them as external realities. You may easily ask: Does this mean that in the spiritual world between death and a new birth, we cannot become aware of what we experience in connection with the other beings and processes of the spiritual world? But then everything is different, we become aware of it differently! Even the seer in the physical world must have what he experiences in the spiritual world reflected by the physical and etheric bodies. This is correct as long as he is living in the physical world, as long as the physical body has not passed away through decay into the physical world and the etheric body through dissolution into the spiritual world. When we are in the spiritual world and no longer have physical and etheric bodies, then we are able, out of what is the substance of the spiritual world, to form the *world of signs* out of which the physical body was put together, and also the world of signs out of which the etheric body was given shape.

Suppose, as a soul between death and a new birth, you are

to live together with another human being. You are aware of this common life. What the other soul says to you or you say to him expresses itself spiritually in such a way that you inscribe into the spiritual world what, in other circumstances, would have been reflected. But now with your own power you inscribe the picture into the spiritual world. What you otherwise express in the signs of the physical and etheric bodies, in vowels or consonants, you now inscribe, you actually inscribe with your own power into the spiritual world, into the Akashic Record, what you are saying to the other soul—obliterating it again, figuratively speaking, when it is no longer needed.

These communications and experiences are to be read and heard in the spiritual world as the result of *mutual* activity on the part of the souls.

I gave the first indications of these things at the beginning of the chapter in my book *Theosophy*, where the so-called 'Spirit-Land' is described. It is there said that at a certain stage of development in Devachan, in the 'Spirit-Land', the human being sees his previous incarnation in the 'Continental Region' of the Spirit-Land. It is an inscription of a spiritual record.

The ideal would be if study of a book like *Theosophy* were so zealous that many a reader, from the indications given there, would arrive at these things for himself. There is a very great deal in these books and merely through one's own reading—if the contents are read with the heart and experienced with deep inwardness—everything can be gleaned from them. But books on Spiritual Science are, as a rule, not read with the attention that they really require. If they *had* been so read, after *Theosophy* and *Knowledge of the Higher Worlds* and perhaps also *Occult Science—an Outline*, had been written, the lecture-courses could have been written or given by someone else than me. Everything, really, is contained in these books, only people do not generally believe it. And how much could be

LECTURE IV

written if everything contained in the Mystery Plays were really to be assimilated! I am not saying this for advertisement's sake—I have already said enough about the humility of the occultist and the spiritual investigator—but I say it in order to stimulate genuine reading of the writings which had to be given out precisely in our epoch, and for which one really has, personally, so little merit.

So you see that the human being, as he lives on the physical plane, develops something in regard to the spiritual worlds which can be a seed for experiences in these higher worlds. The etheric body of man as it is in the physical world is not only his life-principle but it is at the same time an instrument of preparation for unfolding understanding of the vowels of the spiritual world. And the physical body also is an instrument of preparation for experiencing the consonants of the spiritual world.

Much can be done if we try in all earnestness to get rid of the purely materialistic conception of the human physical body. Much can be done in the way of preparation in order that these feelings for the vowels and consonants of the Cosmos, these inner experiences and impulses in the soul may awaken. For this preparation we must call up an experience which, as regards development into the higher worlds, is somewhat similar to what a child must do in order to be able to read in the physical world—what it must do in order to learn the words of our physical language.

With the materialistic conception of the physical body, this body is taken just as it presents itself in the physical sense. It is as though somebody were to write down the signs: I N K ... and then someone comes and says that he will investigate it. This is how we approach the physical body. It is looked at as though it were a scroll with flourishes going up here and down there ... and then it is described. Heart, lung, and so on, are described just as they present themselves externally.

This really is the way it is done. But the only people who get anything out of it are those who have learnt to read the word 'ink' out of the signs.

Thus must we ascend from the physical plane into the higher spiritual worlds with the experiences of which we have spoken to-day. What we learn to read and hear in this way is an individual experience of the soul. But we can prepare if in the physical world we try to comprehend the physical body in its sign-nature. What is meant by this?

I will give you a brief example of understanding this sign-nature. I can do it only very briefly and must leave it to your own earnest meditation to see what is meant. For in many cases speech is not really adequate for understanding these things. It will become adequate only when Spiritual Science has worked for a while in the world and has given the words a stamp which really links them with spiritual activity and spiritual reality. Speech must become more pliant, and this will only be possible when contact with Spiritual Science has been cultivated for some hundreds of years and people have become accustomed to taking words differently from what is the case to-day when they are applied only to things and happenings of the physical plane. Now for the examples.

We find what transpires in the human head to-day enclosed in the bony formation of the skull. There it all is. With a few exceptions it is all physically shut up, as it were, inside. When we begin really to think about the human head, and not merely describe it in its material appearance, we find a tremendous significance in the fact that inside it complicated processes are going on which are shut in practically on all sides by a bony sheath. One part of the physical human being is separated off, surrounded on all sides by the hardest substance, namely that of the bones. It is, however, only a part of the human organism. The human being is by no means a simple entity! The primitiveness of the ideas prevailing at the present time are revealed by the criticisms of my books which grumble at someone who speaks of a Sentient Soul, a Mind-Soul and a Consciousness—or Spiritual Soul, whereas it was a splendid achievement—so it is said—to have been able to conceive of the soul as a unit. It is understandable that our materialistic culture should prefer the hotch-potch that goes by the name of Psychology to-day, to the real membering of the soul. These members of the soul are a reality; they belong to different worlds and are not designated without reason. It is comprehensible that modern culture should consider this foolish, but thereby it simply characterises itself, not what it condemns.

The physical organism of man is highly complicated and study of it may give rise to the following thoughts which may, certainly, seem foolish to those who call themselves scientists to-day. Yes . . . but St. Paul said that much that is wisdom in the eyes of God is foolishness in the eyes of men. And so perhaps it will be profitable to think of this 'foolishness in the eyes of men' which may be 'wisdom in the eyes of God'.

Let us think about the following.—What about our hands? Our hands are quite definitely connected with our soul. If anyone has a living feeling for what goes on in his hands, it is not without significance if what he says to another human being expresses itself in the gestures of his hands. This *means* something in itself! I will pass over many of the intermediate steps, leaving this to your own meditation. Just suppose that as the result, not of a process emanating from the human body, but of a process rooted in the Cosmos, our hands were not formed in such a way that we could move them freely or make them follow our will. Suppose our hands were fettered to our body, were obliged to remain quite rigid, having been affixed to the body, as it were from outside, by external Nature. How would things be then? We should have hands but be unable to move them. But if we had hands and could not use them, we should still have the urge to do so! Although we could not move them physically, we should always be wanting to move the etheric hands! The physical hands would lie still, the etheric hands would move. This, in reality, is what we do with our *brain*. Certain lobes of the brain which now lie enclosed in the skull were freely mobile during the Old Moon evolution. To-day they are rigid and can no longer move physically. But they *do* move etherically, when we *think*. We move the etheric brain when we think. If we had not this firm skull enclosing the lobes of the brain, we should stretch out with these lobes and make gestures with them—gestures such as we now make with the hands—but we should not *think*. The lobes of the brain had first to be made physically rigid and it had to be possible for the etheric brain to tear itself free.

What I am now saying is not fantasy. The time will come when our hands and much else too will become rigid. This will be in the Jupiter epoch. That which to-day appears so free—attached as it were to the heart-region—will then be enclosed by a sheath, just as the brain to-day is enclosed by a skull. That which is most visibly expressed in the hands is something that is preparing to become an organ of thought. For the time being we have only rudimentary organs which at present are small structures because they have not fully developed. Suppose that to-day we had only certain portions of the skull here in front . . . behind there are the shoulder-blades. They lie in the plane which later on will enclose the brain of the future. You have a true conception of the shoulder-blades in the human body when you regard them as small pieces of bone which really belong to a skull that will form—only the other parts have not yet developed. Therewith you have, as it were, added a second man to the first. Moreover—and here I shall say something very strange—there are other organs in the body which are also pieces of *another* skull which will develop in a still more distant future. These organs are

LECTURE IV

now quite tiny compared with the organism as a whole: they are the *knee-caps*. The knee-caps are now these tiny surfaces— mere indications which later on will turn into a different spiritual organ. We characterise the human organism aright if we say (though this is only one isolated example): The human being has, in reality, three skulls. One is fairly well developed, shut off on all sides. The second has only pieces, in the shoulder-blades, the third only in the knee-caps. But the two latter—shoulder-blades and knee-caps—can, in thought, be expanded and rounded off into spherical forms. Thus we get three brains. What we are as inner men is only slightly developed externally in the second brain. To-day it manifests externally; later on it will become an inner brain. When you make gestures with your hands to-day you are preparing for what will be *thoughts* later on—thoughts which will be quite as capable of grasping processes of the elemental world as your head now grasps the processes of the physical world. And strange though it sounds: everything lying outside and beyond the knee-caps, that is to say, the lower legs, the feet—these are still quite imperfect organs connected with the gravity of the Earth. These organs, in conjunction with what they receive spiritually from the Earth to-day, are preparing to become not only physical but spiritual organs, which will lead into the spiritual worlds when the Earth is replaced by the later Venus evolution. The present physical form must fall away and something else take its place.

So you see; much, very much is contained in the occult study of the world. The most important is not that we know: This or that book exists and contains this and that concerning the higher worlds. That is not the most important. What the books contain must, naturally, be assimilated because that is the only way of finding what is right and true. But the necessary thing is a certain 'temper' of the soul, whereby a man relates himself in a new way to the world, whereby he learns to have a different view of the things of the world. The important thing is that by this reading we prepare for the inner mobility and movement of the life of thought, for the weaving of thought, for the experience of thought-in-itself; that we also prepare to see the physical world in a different way. For even in their outer form things are not as they seem. Strange as it sounds, the shoulder-blade is not what you see physically. That it has such definite limits is Maya, is false. The shoulder-blade expands, when we really set about comprehending it, into an organ with much greater detail. And when we see a man kneeling, we should gradually get the impression: That is a false picture! The knee-caps there, those tiny parts, are illusory; this kneeling man is surrounded by a great spherical surface and he lives within that orb. The surface becomes a sphere and when a man prays he is preparing himself in the brain to live in the sphere in which he will live when the sphere of which the knee-caps are only tiny parts, encloses him.

Thus we gradually learn to read in the physical world. We do not merely look at a man kneeling or making some gesture, but we begin to realise that although what presents itself immediately, is reality, none the less it is false and untrue. In the 'letters' we learn what the Cosmos is, not only in the present but what it expresses in its 'Becoming'. A man in prayer becomes, in his form, what the Venus man will sometime be. Thus do we learn, step by step, to decipher, interpret, read in the true sense, and grasp the world as it really is. The physical world is no more than a written page before us. If we only stare at it, we can observe it without being able to *read* it at all. Neither do we know anything of the world if we look at it merely with the faculty of physical perception, for then we do not decipher, we do not really penetrate into the world. We must *read* the world, learn its meaning.

If we become more and more conscious that the world is a

book which the Hierarchies have written for us, in order that we may read in it, then only do we become *Man* in the full sense of the word. The building on which we are working is intended in its form to draw out those feelings and intimate moods of soul which make us capable of reading the world and of hearing the secrets of the Universe. The building is as it is in order that it may draw out what is within us—a certain part, at least.

It is good, my dear friends, to make a picture in our meditations of the task which Spiritual Science has in the world over against what is in the world to-day; it is good to picture what must develop out of Spiritual Science and how Spiritual Science must find its way into the further development of history.

If only there could be in the Anthroposophical Society a body of human beings filled with the living consciousness that Spiritual Science has to be worked and woven into the evolution of humanity!

It was not merely in order to impart truths to you, but to stimulate such feelings in your souls, my dear friends, that I have given these lectures.

Relevant literature

By Rudolf Steiner:
Theosophy. An Introduction to the Supersensible Knowledge of the World and the Destination of Man
Knowledge of the Higher Worlds. How is it achieved?
Occult Science—An Outline
Guidance in Esoteric Training
The Threshold of the Spiritual World
Human and Cosmic Thought
True and False Paths in Spiritual Investigation
Macrocosm and Microcosm
The Spiritual Hierarchies and their Reflection in the Physical World
Supersensible Man
Man in the Light of Occultism, Theosophy and Philosophy
The Mission of the Individual Folk Souls
Links Between the Living and the Dead
Practical Training in Thinking

All the published works of Rudolf Steiner in print in English translation as well as the works of other authors on Anthroposophy can be obtained from Rudolf Steiner Press, 35 Park Road, London NW1 6XT. Catalogue available.

COMPLETE EDITION

of the works of Rudolf Steiner in the original German. Published by the *Rudolf Steiner Nachlassverwaltung*, Dornach, Switzerland, by whom all rights are reserved.

General Plan (abbreviated):

A. WRITINGS

I. Works written between 1883 and 1925
II. Essays and articles written between 1882 and 1925
III. Letters, drafts, manuscripts, fragments, verses, inscriptions, meditative sayings, etc.

B. LECTURES

I. Public Lectures
II. Lectures to Members of the Anthroposophical Society on general anthroposophical subjects
   Lectures to Members on the history of the Anthroposophical Movement and Anthroposophical Society
III. Lectures and Courses on special branches of work:
   Art: Eurythmy, Speech and Drama, Music, Visual Arts, History of Art
   Education
   Medicine and Therapy
   Science
   Sociology and the Threefold Social Order
   Lectures given to Workmen at the Goetheanum

The total number of lectures amounts to some six thousand, shorthand reports of which are available in the case of the great majority.

C. REPRODUCTIONS and SKETCHES

Paintings in water colour, drawings, coloured diagrams, Eurythmy forms, etc.

When the Edition is complete the total number of volumes, each of a considerable size, will amount to several hundreds. A full and detailed *Bibliographical Survey*, with subjects, dates and places where the lectures were given, is available.

All the volumes can be obtained from the Rudolf Steiner Press in London as well as directly from the *Rudolf Steiner Nachlassverwaltung* (address as above).